Sutton, Felix C.1

Indian chiefs
of the West

DATE		

INDIAN CHIEFS OF THE WEST

BOOKS BY FELIX SUTTON

INDIAN CHIEFS OF THE WEST

SONS OF LIBERTY

BIG GAME HUNTER: *Carl Akeley*

DANIEL BOONE

DISCOVERERS OF AMERICA

HOW AND WHY WONDER BOOK OF THE
AMERICAN REVOLUTION

VALIANT VIRGINIAN: *Stonewall Jackson*

WE WERE THERE AT THE BATTLE OF
LEXINGTON AND CONCORD

INDIAN CHIEFS OF THE WEST

By FELIX SUTTON

ILLUSTRATED BY
RUSSELL HOOVER

JULIAN MESSNER   NEW YORK

Published simultaneously in the United States and Canada by
Julian Messner, a division of Simon & Schuster, Inc.,
1 West 39 Street, New York, N.Y. 10018. All rights reserved.

Printed in the United States of America
SBN 671-32254-O Cloth Trade
671-32255-9 MCE

Library of Congress Catalog Card No. 70—107062

DESIGN : LEON KOTKOFSKY

For all the Indians of the West

oᴄ⊃o

CONTENTS

〜〜〜〜〜〜〜〜〜

INDIAN CHIEFS OF THE WEST

THE PLAINS INDIANS

INTRODUCTION

〜〜〜〜〜〜〜〜〜〜

THE PLAINS INDIANS

———◆———

THE WINNING OF THE AMERICAN WEST WAS PROBABLY the most important, and certainly the most adventurous, chapter in our country's stormy history. It made possible the expansion of a young and restless United States out to the wide and fertile Plains beyond the Mississippi River—and farther to the western mountains that were rich in iron ore, copper, and gold.

The settlement of the American West created a great and powerful nation that was three times bigger than it had been before. And it made the United States into the most productive and prosperous country the world has ever known.

For the most part, this was a period of bitter and bloody warfare between the white immigrants and the Plains Indians, a cruel war that went on for almost fifty years.

It was a war in which both sides sincerely believed that they were right. The Indians thought of the white men as intruders who were invading their age-old hunting grounds. This was true. The white men looked upon the Indians as savages who were standing in the way of America's progress—as indeed they were.

The Indian tribes of the Great Plains depended upon the buffalo for almost all their needs. In herds of tens of thousands, these great beasts covered the flat prairie land like a huge moving carpet of brown. Aside from a few antelope, deer, and elk, some game birds and wild vegetables, buffalo meat was the Indians' only food. They made their clothes, moccasins, leggings, ropes, and the covering for their teepees from its hide. Its horns were carved into spoons and dishes. Its hoofs were boiled to make glue. From the buffalo's bones, the Indians fashioned needles and other tools. They used its sinews for thread and bowstrings. In those parts of the

Plains where there was very little wood, slabs of sun-dried buffalo dung, called chips, served as fuel for the cooking fires.

Unlike the tribes of the East and far Northwest, most of the Plains Indians had no permanent villages. They moved their teepee encampments from place to place to follow the buffalo herds grazing over the grasslands. To the Indians, the buffalo was sacred. They slaughtered only as many as they needed, and they never made the slightest dent in the buffalo's great numbers. Whenever a buffalo was killed, the Indians thanked it and called it "brother," and turned its skull to face the rising sun.

On the other hand, the American emigrants from the East felt that the big, broad, untouched lands of the West were going to waste. The soil was black, loamy, and rich, perfect for the fields of wheat and corn that would one day stretch from horizon to horizon. The thick, knee-high sweet grass was just right for the huge herds of cattle that could be fattened for markets in the Eastern cities.

The white migration westward began a few years after President Thomas Jefferson bought the Northwest country from the French in 1803. This was included in the Louisiana Purchase, and it extended the boundaries of the United States all the way west to the Pacific Ocean.

A thin trickle of covered-wagon trains began to flow out through the Indian lands after the Lewis and Clark Expedition brought back glowing reports of the richness of this new land. The trickle became a steady stream when gold was discovered in California in 1849. And it swelled to a mighty flood at the end of the Civil

Introduction: THE PLAINS INDIANS

War after Congress had passed the first Homestead Act.

This law gave every American citizen the right to stake out a farm or a ranch on lands that the Plains Indians had always considered to be their own. These lands, called the Great Plains, reached from the eastern base of the Rocky Mountains to the Mississippi River. The United States government offered to pay the Indian tribes for their land, but it never got around to doing so.

It has been said that the white man's trail across the West was littered with broken promises. The U.S. Army and the Agency for Indian Affairs made dozens of treaties with the tribes, guaranteeing them that their lands would be forever free. But whenever it suited the officials in Washington, these treaties were broken.

Homesteaders swarmed onto the Plains, fenced them in, plowed them, and planted their crops. In so doing, they drove the buffalo away. Cattlemen ran the buffalo off the range to make room for their beef herds. And they too fenced in large areas with barbed wire.

But the railroads and the hide-hunters were the worst buffalo-destroyers of all.

As the twin lines of steel rails stretched across the Plains, the track-laying crews needed hundreds of tons of buffalo meat each week for food. Professional hunters were hired to slaughter them. The famous Buffalo Bill

Cody alone killed 4,862 of the magnificent animals in a single summer.

When buffalo coats and buffalo robes became fashionable in the East, hide-hunters shot down the big beasts by the tens of thousands. It was a senseless killing, for the hunters took only the skins and left the bare carcasses to rot under the broiling prairie sun.

Slowly but surely, the Indians found their hunting grounds shrinking and their way of life disappearing. They had no choice but to fight back. To protect the settlers, the United States Army set up a line of forts along the main routes to the West—the Oregon Trail, the Santa Fe Trail, and the Bozeman Trail. Scattered fights took place and many brave men, both red and white, were killed.

In general, the Indians called American soldiers Blue Coats because of the color of their uniforms. They referred to the cavalry as Horse Soldiers, and to the infantry as Walk-a-Heaps. After the Civil War, a great many freed Negro slaves joined the Army of the West. The Indians called them Buffalo Soldiers, because their black, close-cropped, thickly curling hair reminded them of buffalo fur. The Buffalo Soldiers were proud of this name because they knew the Indians meant it as a great compliment.

Introduction: *THE PLAINS INDIANS*

As a rule, the white settlers and most Army officers tried to deal fairly with the Indians. But the government in Washington—the Agency for Indian Affairs, in particular—cheated them, lied to them, stole from them, and broke the treaties they had made with them. While the winning of the West was an important and adventurous period in our country's history, it was, from the standpoint of the government's treatment of the Plains tribes, also the most shameful.

The Plains Indians were fighting for a doomed cause. They did not have the slightest chance of winning against the power of the United States Army and the great flood of westward migration. But for nearly half a century, they put up one of the toughest fights that any army in the world has ever been faced with.

In their long and hopeless struggle to survive, many great leaders rose up among the tribes. This is the story of five of the most famous Indian chiefs of the West.

One of them, Sequoyah, was a genius and an educator. He took no part in the fight against the white men because it did not become serious until after his life's work was finished. But no book about Western Indian chiefs would be complete without him.

Two of them, Chief Joseph and Sitting Bull, were men of peace who were forced to become men of war.

The final two, Crazy Horse and Geronimo, were fierce fighters who struggled to drive the palefaces out of their ancient lands once and for all.

CHAPTER ONE

SEQUOYAH

THE CHEROKEE GENIUS

IN STATUARY HALL OF THE CAPITOL BUILDING AT Washington, D.C., the states of the Union are represented by statues of their most distinguished sons. Of all the great men of American history whose images stand in this Hall of Fame, only one is an Indian. He is honored by the state of Oklahoma, and his name is Sequoyah. He was an uneducated Cherokee who could neither read, speak, nor write English, and who started out in life as a repairer of pots and pans.

SEQUOYAH

Chapter One: SEQUOYAH

The largest living things on earth are a species of redwood tree that grows in California. These trees are called sequoyahs or *sequoias*, after the great chief.

Why has the memory of this quiet and unassuming Indian been so widely honored? It is because he was one of the true native geniuses of all time.

He was the only man in the entire history of the human race who, alone and without any help, devised and perfected a complete system for writing and reading a language.

Our own written language, English, has come down to us from the Phoenicians, the Greeks, and the Romans. It slowly took shape over tens of centuries. But Sequoyah created a written Indian language in just about ten years.

At the time of Sequoyah's birth, there were many different languages and dialects used by the Indians. Sometimes a tribe living in one river valley was entirely ignorant of the language spoken by a tribe that lived in another valley perhaps only a few miles away.

There was no such thing as Indian writing. Although the language of the Indians was a simple one, it consisted of thousands of sounds. These were put together in a manner that was very melodious and pleasing to the ear, and not in a series of grunts or "ughs" as so many people wrongfully suppose. This way of speaking comes down to us in such rhythmic and tuneful Indian names as Mississippi, Tennessee, Shenandoah, Ohio, Oklahoma, Suwanee, and Allegheny. And a great many of our modern everyday words are pure Indian—hickory, succotash, moose, raccoon, and squash.

Sequoyah was born in eastern Tennessee, in the high ridges of the Great Smoky Mountains, in either 1775 or 1776. No accurate birth records were kept in those days, especially among the Indians. Sequoyah preferred 1776 because that was also the birth year of the United States. His father was a white trader named Nathaniel Gist, the son of a prominent Maryland family. His mother was Wut-teh, daughter of a Cherokee chief. His own English name was George Gist (sometimes written in old documents as George Guess or George Guest), but he never used it. He was too fiercely proud of being an Indian.

Every Indian name has a specific meaning, and Sequoyah meant "The Lame One" in the Cherokee tongue. He had walked with a limp since he was a small boy, probably because of a childhood bone disease.

He grew up on a fine mountain farm where most of the hard work was done by Negro slaves. The young Sequoyah resented his white blood, as he was to all through his lifetime. He insisted that he was all Indian. He spoke Cherokee, a little Choctaw, and Mobilian. The latter was an extremely simple trade-language, a sort of baby-talk that had been developed when the first white settlers and traders had come over the mountains many years before. Sequoyah refused to learn to speak English, and he would not go to the white man's school.

His grandfather, the old chief, was a skilled wood-carver whose clever hands created ceremonial masks for the tribe's dances; spoons, bowls, dishes, and spinning looms for the Cherokee women; and bows and arrows for the hunters. The boy Sequoyah first began working with wood as his grandfather did. Then he became fascinated with the metalsmith's art. From a traveling English tinker who could speak Mobilian, he learned how to build and operate a small forge, how to mend iron and copper cookware, and how to hammer out bracelets and other ornaments from pieces of silver. It was as a silversmith and coppersmith that he earned his living for the rest of his life.

When Sequoyah was nineteen or twenty, he married a full-blooded Cherokee girl and settled down to raise a family. With his farm work and his trade of metalworking, he made a good living for his wife and children.

Then came the War of 1812, in which the English

attempted to win back the American colonies which
they had lost in the Revolution. Along with many other
Cherokees, Sequoyah volunteered for service with the
United States Army.

Actually, the Cherokees had no great interest in the
war. Safely behind their shield of mountain walls, they
felt that the fighting among the white men was no con-
cern of theirs. But the tribes of the Creek Confederacy,

who lived to the south in Georgia, and who were ene-mies of the Cherokees, had taken sides with the British. The Cherokees saw this as an opportunity to settle an ancient quarrel. Besides, the Cherokees were discussing a new series of treaties with the government in Wash-ington to preserve their age-old lands for themselves. They decided that if they lined up with the Americans against the British and the Creeks, they might get bet-ter treatment from the officials in Washington.

So, at the age of thirty-six or thirty-seven, Sequoyah shouldered his flintlock musket, filled his war bag, and rode off to join the Army.

It was during his war service that Sequoyah was struck by the brilliant, and completely unheard-of, idea which was to stamp him forever with the mark of genius.

In Army camps, an Indian soldier or scout had to wait for a chance meeting with a friend from his na-tive village before he could get news from home. On the other hand, the white soldiers received letters—marks on a piece of paper—that somehow spoke to them. In return, the white men wrote back to their families on paper or thin sheets of birch bark. Sequoyah called these letters the "talking leaves," and got to wondering about them.

He reasoned that each mark in the white man's writing stood for a sound. If you recognized the mark, you could translate it in your mind into that sound. And in this way you could go on to build words and sentences.

When the war was finally over, and the United States had finally won, Sequoyah could not get the idea of the "talking leaves" out of his head. Why, he kept asking himself, couldn't the Cherokees find a way to communicate with each other in writing? The more he pondered this mystery, the more determined he became that it could be done. Back in his Tennessee mountain home, he grew so interested in the idea of writing that he lost all interest in his work as a farmer and metalsmith. He now had four big sons who could run the farm and take charge of the slaves. So he began to spend all of his time sitting in front of the kitchen fire scrawling marks on pieces of birch bark with a charcoal crayon.

His wife had no understanding of what he was trying to do. To her, it seemed that he only wanted to loaf instead of work. At last one day, in a sudden fit of rage, she scooped up all his writings and threw them into the fire. She called him a lazy, no-good white man (an insult to any Indian), and left him to go back to her own people. His sons stayed to work the farm. With his small daughter, Ah-yoka, Sequoyah retired to a small cabin back in the woods. There he devoted every hour of every day working with the problem of the "talking leaves."

Slowly, a written Cherokee language began to take form. In the beginning, Sequoyah tried to design a mark, or sign, for every one of the thousands of sounds in his spoken language. Then, by trial and error, he began to throw out some and combine others until he had simplified his writing system to eighty-six basic characters. Using these eighty-six signs, just as we use the twenty-six letters in our English alphabet, any thought or idea in the Cherokee tongue could be written as well as spoken.

Strictly speaking, Sequoyah's method of writing was not an alphabet. Instead it was a "syllabary"—that is, the signs represented syllables rather than letters. Thus, if Sequoyah wrote the word "cornfield" as it was pronounced in the Cherokee language, he used not nine letters but only two syllables.

After the War of 1812, a great number of Cherokees had migrated from the hills of the East to the broad new lands of the West. There they had formed what they called the Western Cherokee Nation. Sequoyah decided that he should join them, if only to make sure

CHEROKEE ALPHABET.

Characters as arranged by the inventor.

Ꭱ Ꭰ Ꮃ Ꮵ Ꮐ Ꮽ Ꮺ Ꮅ Ꮑ Ꮌ Ꭹ Ᏹ Ꮟ Ꮲ Ꭳ Ꮇ Ꮄ Ꭽ Ꮼ Ꮰ Ꮤ Ᏼ Ꮈ Ꭿ Ꮝ

Ᏺ Ꮁ Ꭺ Ꮷ Ꮍ Ꮞ Ꮠ Ꮯ Ꮘ Ꮗ Ꮜ Ꮖ Ꮓ Ꭷ Ꮸ Ꮢ Ꮒ Ꭶ Ꮩ Ꭸ Ꮣ Ꭼ Ꮻ Ꭲ Ꭴ

Ᏸ Ꮂ Ꮫ Ꭻ Ꮶ Ꮙ Ꮔ Ꮎ Ꮆ Ᏻ Ꮴ Ꮧ Ꮾ Ꮪ Ꮥ Ꮳ Ꭵ Ꮕ Ꮦ Ꮉ Ꮡ Ꮱ Ꭾ Ꮀ Ꮋ

Ꮭ Ꮿ Ꮹ Ꮨ Ꮮ Ꮏ Ꮚ Ꮬ Ꮊ Ꮛ.

Characters systematically arranged with the sounds.

	Ꭰ a	Ꭱ e	Ꭲ i	Ꭳ o	Ꭴ u	Ꭵ v
	Ꭶ ga Ꭷ ka	Ꭸ ge	Ꭹ gi	Ꭺ go	Ꭻ gu	Ꭼ gv
	Ꭽ ha	Ꭾ he	Ꭿ hi	Ꮀ ho	Ꮁ hu	Ꮂ hv
	Ꮃ la	Ꮄ le	Ꮅ li	Ꮆ lo	Ꮇ lu	Ꮈ lv
	Ꮉ ma	Ꮊ me	Ꮋ mi	Ꮌ mo	Ꮍ mu	
	Ꮎ na Ꮏ hna Ꮐ nah	Ꮑ ne	Ꮒ ni	Ꮓ no	Ꮔ nu	Ꮕ nv
	Ꮖ qua	Ꮗ que	Ꮘ qui	Ꮙ quo	Ꮚ quu	Ꮛ quv
Ꮝ s	Ꮜ sa	Ꮞ se	Ꮟ si	Ꮠ so	Ꮡ su	Ꮢ sv
	Ꮣ da Ꮤ ta	Ꮥ de Ꮦ te	Ꮧ di Ꮨ ti	Ꮩ do	Ꮪ du	Ꮫ dv
	Ꮬ dla Ꮭ tla	Ꮮ tle	Ꮯ tli	Ꮰ tlo	Ꮱ tlu	Ꮲ tlv
	Ꮳ tsa	Ꮴ tse	Ꮵ tsi	Ꮶ tso	Ꮷ tsu	Ꮸ tsv
	Ꮹ wa	Ꮺ we	Ꮻ wi	Ꮼ wo	Ꮽ wu	Ꮾ wv
	Ꮿ ya	Ᏸ ye	Ᏹ yi	Ᏺ yo	Ᏻ yu	Ᏼ yv

Sounds represented by vowels.

a as *a* in *father*, or short as *a* in *rival*,
e as *a* in *hate*, or short as *e* in *met*,
i as *i* in *pique*, or short as *i* in *pit*,
o as *aw* in *law*, or short as *o* in *not*,
u as *oo* in *fool*, or short as *u* in *pull*,
v as *u* in *but*, nasalized.

Consonant sounds.

g nearly as in English, but approaching to k. d nearly as in English, but approaching to t. h, k, l, m, n, q, s, t, w, y, as in English.

Syllables beginning with g, except Ꭶ, have sometimes the power of k. Ꭳ, Ꮪ, Ꮫ, are sometimes sounded to, tu, tv; and syllables written with tl, except Ꮭ, sometimes vary to dl.

Courtesy, Thomas Gilcrease Institute of American History and Art

Sequoyah's Syllabary

that his new written language could be understood by Cherokees everywhere. Transferring his writings from the original slabs of birch bark to pieces of finely tanned deerskin, he and Ah-yoka started out on their long journey. He paid their way by taking up once more his old trade of pot-repairer and silversmith.

Along the way, Sequoyah met a young Cherokee woman named Sally, who had a small son and whose husband had been killed in the war. They decided to get married, and now Sequoyah was a family man again. The four continued westward, by wagon and river flatboat, until they came to the Oklahoma Territory. There Sequoyah staked out a small farm for himself near what is now the town of Sallisaw, in Sequoyah County.

In their new home, Sequoyah worked on his farm and at his trade during the days, and perfected his Cherokee syllabary in the evenings. With Sally, Ah-yoka and his stepson, Squirrel Boy, he made it into a family game. All four of them practiced reading and writing. They would compose sentences when one of them was out of the room, and then have that person read the page when he came back in.

By the year 1821, Sequoyah felt that he had his written language so nearly perfect that he could present it to the Cherokee Tribal Council, the assembly of all the

important chiefs in the Cherokee Nation.

His presentation to the chiefs was quietly dramatic. He employed the same method that he had used with Sally and the children.

"I will leave the room," he told the chiefs. "Then you can tell Ah-yoka what to write on a piece of paper.

When she has done this, I will return and read what she has written."

As soon as Sequoyah had stepped outside—he took a long walk to calm his nerves—the chiefs dictated a message to the girl, who wrote it down as her father had taught her. When she was finished, Sequoyah was called back. Taking the paper from her hand, he read it clearly and accurately.

The assembled chiefs could hardly believe that such a thing was possible. After a moment of astonished silence, they crowded around Sequoyah and began to cheer.

At last the Cherokees had a written language all their own. At last they could write letters to their friends. At last they could publish newspapers and books that every Cherokee could read.

Within a few years, Sequoyah's new system of writing had been adopted by all Cherokee schools, and all children—as well as most grownups—learned to read and write it. The Bible was printed in Cherokee characters. The Indians established their own newspaper, which was circulated throughout the Cherokee Nation, both East and West.

Sequoyah himself became the most famous and honored of all the Cherokees. He was elected a chief, given a lifetime pension by his grateful people, and represented the Nation in its dealings with the United States government in Washington.

But whenever he had occasion to sign his name to an official document, he did not write it as George Gist— for he still had not learned to read or write in English.

Nor did he wish to.

Instead he always signed in the Cherokee characters he had created:

CHAPTER TWO

CRAZY HORSE

WAR CHIEF OF THE SIOUX

EXCEPT FOR HIS BRIEF SERVICE IN THE ARMY DURING the War of 1812, in which he did little if any fighting, Sequoyah's life was largely that of a quiet scholar. But for most of the other Western Indian chiefs of the nineteenth century, life was a never-ending battle for survival against the white intruders who wanted their lands.

This was especially true in the case of Crazy Horse. At first he fought the white soldiers with every trick that his brilliant brain could think of. But defeated by the overpowering numbers and superior weapons of the United States Army, he tried to make friends with them. It was then he discovered that the white man was just as deadly to his friends as to his enemies.

Crazy Horse was born, about 1840, into the Oglala Sioux, a buffalo-hunting tribe that roamed over the Dakotas and western Wyoming. His father was a medicine man. As far as anyone knows, Crazy Horse had no white blood, but his complexion was fairer than that of most Indians, and his hair was dark brown instead of coal black. For this reason his mother named him Has-ka, which meant "light-skinned."

From the time Has-ka was a very small boy, he was determined that one day he would be a great warrior, perhaps even a chief. He spent all his time perfecting his skills at war games and hunting. Since the horse played such an important part in the lives of the Plains Indians, every Sioux youth had to be an expert rider. But of all the Oglala, Has-ka was easily the best.

The Sioux name for a mustang—the wild horses that roamed the Great Plains—was *tashunka-witko*, meaning crazy horse. These horses were the descendants of those that had escaped from the Spanish Conquistadores three centuries before. Now they grazed in great

CRAZY HORSE

numbers over the prairies. The Indians roped them and
gentled them. They rode bareback; their bridle was a
single short length of rawhide looped around the horse's
lower jaw. Sometimes they made primitive saddles
from the hide of a buffalo or the skin of a mountain
sheep.

Because mustangs did not usually live long in cap-
tivity—and particularly because the chief pleasure of
a band of Plains Indians was stealing horses from an
enemy tribe—the horse herds had to be renewed every
year by a roundup of wild ones.

When he was about twelve, Has-ka, riding one of his
father's ponies, went out with the older braves on the
annual horse-hunt. Coming upon a mustang herd, Has-
ka's trained eye picked out the biggest and best-looking
stallion in the group. As the wild horses moved around
in confusion, Has-ka managed to slip the loop of his
lasso—a rawhide rope attached to a long cottonwood
stick—over the stallion's head, half-choking him. In
this way, he led the gasping horse to a nearby river
that was deep enough for swimming.

In midstream, the boy jumped from his own pony
and scrambled onto the stallion's back. As he did so, he
loosened the noose. After half an hour or so in the
water, long enough to get the horse accustomed to the

feeling of a rider on its back, Has-ka turned him toward the shore. By this time the stallion was tired out
and seemed almost subdued. However, when he was
back on dry land, he bucked and reared for a few
minutes. But he soon gave up and went along quietly.

The big stallion was the finest horse that had been
captured that day. When Has-ka returned to camp, his
father proclaimed to all the tribe: "Has-ka has ridden
the best of the crazy horses. From now on he will have

a name more fitting for an Oglala brave than Light-Skinned. He will be called Tashunka-Witko—Crazy Horse!"

Crazy Horse's first brush with the white man's cruelty came only a few weeks later. His mother had been a Brulé Sioux, a band closely related to the Oglala. One hot summer day he rode his new stallion over to the Brulé encampment to visit his uncles, aunts, and cousins.

A few days before, a wagon train of immigrants had left a sick and dying cow on the trail. A Sioux had killed her for her hide. When the commander at nearby Fort Laramie discovered this, he sent out an infantry company to arrest the Indian. They were commanded by a young lieutenant, just out of West Point, named J. L. Grattan.

When Grattan strode into the Indian camp, he was met by two Brulé chiefs, an old man named Stirring Bear and a younger one who was called Man-Afraid-of-His-Horses. The young chief had not been given his name because he was afraid of his own horses. It was because he was such a fierce fighter that his enemies became frightened by the mere sight of any horses that belonged to him.

The two chiefs explained that the cow would have

died in a day or two anyway. They offered to give the immigrants three good horses in payment for the animal in order to avoid trouble.

Grattan refused to listen to any explanations. He walked back to his soldiers and ordered them to open fire upon the Indians. As the first rifle slugs ripped into the Brulé camp, a bullet struck Stirring Bear in the chest and killed him. The Indians returned the fire with a shower of arrows and shots from the few ancient guns they owned.

Young Crazy Horse was at first astounded. Then he grabbed his bow and joined in the fight. Grattan tried to retreat, but on his way back to the fort he ran into a

party of angry Oglala. Within minutes, he and all of his men lay dead on the bloodstained buffalo grass of the prairie.

The "Grattan Massacre," as the Eastern newspapers called the affair, set off dozens of Army raids on Indian camps. Naturally, the tribes struck back. They attacked wagon trains, stagecoaches, small Army detachments, and the farms and ranches of white settlers. Crazy Horse, who was now growing into young manhood, joined in these raids and soon became known as a fearless and reckless—but very intelligent—warrior. Having seen with his own eyes how the whites had broken their promises to the Indian people, he swore that he would never quit fighting until all white men had been driven out of Indian country.

Then, in 1865, after the Civil War had come to an end, the Army and the Indian Agency offered the Plains tribes a treaty which at long last appeared to be a good one. It guaranteed the Sioux, the Cheyenne, and the Arapaho all of what was then known as the Powder River Country. This included all the lands that lay between the Black Hills, the Yellowstone River, and the Rocky Mountains. These were the finest buffalo-hunting grounds on the Plains. In addition, the Black Hills were sacred to the Sioux as the ancestral home of their gods. The white leaders solemnly promised that these lands would belong exclusively to the Indians "as long as the rivers ran and the grass grew."

Meanwhile, in spite of the fact that he was a very young man, Crazy Horse had been chosen by his people as a subchief. In his heart he did not believe that the United States government would live up to its treaty. He decided to train his own Oglala warriors in the art of war as he had seen it practiced by the Blue Coats.

The Plains Indians had always fought as individuals, for personal glory. But Crazy Horse had seen that the American soldiers fought in groups, with a plan of attack and defense. Although most of the Oglala warriors grumbled at these new tactics, Crazy Horse began to train them in his own way.

Before a year had passed, the young Chief's fears about the white man's treaty became true. Gold was discovered in Idaho and Montana, and a new wave of immigrants came pouring into the Powder River Country. The Indian Agency in Washington now wanted to make a second treaty that would allow them to build a new road and a string of protective forts through the Indian lands. The chiefs refused. Both Crazy Horse and the aging Chief Red Cloud warned the commander at Fort Laramie, Colonel Henry B. Carrington, that "the time has come for either peace or war."

The officials in Washington now found themselves backed into an awkward corner. They had to either fight the Indians openly or keep their own citizens out of the Indian lands by force. The decision was obvious. Colonel Carrington was ordered to build a road, the Bozeman Trail, squarely through the Powder River Country to Montana, and to construct a line of forts to protect it. The first base he built was Fort Phil Kearny.

Warfare flamed up again. Crazy Horse and his braves began ambushing wagon trains, making quick attacks against the fort, and picking off small parties of cavalry and infantry whenever they caught them out alone on patrol.

While this hit-and-run war was going on, Crazy

Horse was busy putting together an army of about a thousand Arapaho, Cheyenne, Hunkpapa, and Miniconjou Sioux, plus about as many Oglala. He was training them in his new fighting strategy.

A few days before Christmas of 1866, he baited a trap.

Fort Phil Kearny was surrounded by an open area of treeless prairie. The nearest stand of timber that could be used for firewood was five or six miles away. Once every week or two, a woodcutting party, guarded by a squad of cavalry, took a train of wagons into the timber.

On this particular morning, Crazy Horse hid his fighters along both sides of a narrow, rocky ravine. Then he sent out a small party of a dozen braves to take potshots at the train when it was a couple of miles from the fort. When the cavalry saw the Indians coming, one trooper raced back to the fort shouting the warning: "Many Injuns!"

Colonel Carrington at once sent a relief party of eighty-one cavalrymen to rescue the men in the wood-cutting train. The relief party was commanded by Captain William Fetterman. The Colonel gave Fetterman firm orders to relieve the train, bring it in, but "under no circumstances go in pursuit of the Indians."

But Captain Fetterman was new to the frontier, and was full of fight. He had often loudly boasted that with eighty veteran troopers he could clean out the whole Sioux Nation, and the Cheyenne and Arapaho as well. Now he had one man more than eighty, and he could not wait any longer.

Disregarding his orders, Fetterman charged his men past the wood train and went after the dozen Indian braves—right into the ambush that Crazy Horse had set up. Yelling their war cry—*"Hoka-hey!" (Let's go!)*—Crazy Horse's braves snapped shut the jaws of the trap. Firing from behind rocks and dirt dunes, the troopers put up a good fight. But in half an hour or less it was all over. Fetterman's command had been killed to the last man.

The fighting continued throughout the winter and into the next summer. Then, unexpectedly, news came from Washington over the "talking wire" (as the Indians called the telegraph line) that the American government wanted to make a new Powder River treaty. Crazy Horse, Sitting Bull (chief of the Hunkpapa Sioux), and their fellow chiefs stood firm. They would sign only if the Army agreed to close down all the forts along the Powder River and leave the land to the Indians. The Indian Agency gave in. The forts were abandoned. After the last of the Blue Coats had marched away, Crazy Horse ordered that all the stockades be burned to the ground.

For the next few years, the white man's struggle to control the Great Plains raged all around the edges of the Powder River Country. Then came the final blow. The Black Hills had up to now been considered worthless to the white homesteaders and ranchers. But in 1874, a few daring prospectors had ventured into the holy country of the Sioux and discovered gold. Almost overnight, another tide of white men flooded into the hills. Again, it was time for the government in Washington to break the Powder River treaty.

Orders went out that all the Plains Indians must come in and live on reservations. Much money was offered to the tribes for the rights to the land, money which the U.S. government would never pay. The Indians were warned that whoever did not come to the reservations of his own free will would be considered "hostile" and would be hunted down and killed like a dangerous animal.

Many of the old chiefs, including Red Cloud of the Oglala, decided that further fighting was hopeless. And so they surrendered. The Indian Agency treated Red Cloud, who had once been a great leader, with much respect. They even named the Red Cloud Reservation in his honor. This influenced hundreds of Sioux to give themselves up and come in peacefully.

But Crazy Horse, who was now head chief of the Oglala, and Sitting Bull, withdrew into the hills to carry on the fight for their freedom. Crazy Horse kept most of his army together, and more fighting braves gathered around him.

In the summer of 1876, a force of 3,000 to 4,000 hand-picked veterans—Horse Soldiers, Buffalo Soldiers and Walk-a-Heaps — moved into the Powder River Country with orders to find Crazy Horse's army and wipe it out once and for all. This expedition was commanded by General George Crook.

Crook's most dashing officer was Lieutenant Colonel George Armstrong Custer, who had been a boy-hero of the Civil War. The Indians called him Long Hair because his flowing curls swept down over the shoulders of his fringed buckskin jacket.

When Crook pressed deeply into Indian country, he sent Custer and his Seventh Cavalry to scout ahead and locate the positions of Crazy Horse and Sitting Bull. Crook carefully instructed Custer not to attack until the rest of the Army could come up to support him.

Custer found the Indians in the valley of the Little Big Horn River. Having been in the West for nearly ten years, Custer should have known better—but, like Fetterman, he disobeyed his orders. With visions of glory dancing in his head, he ordered the Seventh forward.

What he didn't know—and didn't bother to find out, as any careful commander should have—was that

Chapter Two: CRAZY HORSE

Crazy Horse and Sitting Bull had set up another of their traps. The Indians that Custer saw were only a small body of braves. Crazy Horse had his main force hidden behind in the hills. When Custer's force had been drawn into the jaws of the pincers, Crazy Horse's warriors came down on them from all sides. Custer tried to retreat toward the safety of the top of a hill, but the Indians occupied it. Custer was forced to fight on the hillside. The battle that the Seventh put up against overwhelming odds did not last long. When the final rifle shot and the last arrow had been slung, the whole of the Seventh Cavalry—264 officers and men, including George Armstrong Custer—lay dead on the side of the hill.

After the victory over Custer, the Indians knew that the United States Army would be without pity in its search for revenge. Crazy Horse and Sitting Bull decided that the best thing would be to break up their forces and scatter. Sitting Bull took his Sioux northward into Canada. Crazy Horse led his Oglala deeper into the Black Hills.

Then came the sad news that Red Cloud and some of the older chiefs had at last sold the Black Hills. They had given up all the Indians' rights to their sacred hunting grounds. Regiments of American cavalry were searching for bands of Sioux and either capturing or killing them.

The weather was below zero. Buffalo and antelope were scarce. The Oglala began to starve. A half-breed runner who was a scout for the Army got through to Crazy Horse with a message from General Crook. If Crazy Horse would agree to surrender, the runner said, all the Oglala would be treated well.

Crazy Horse looked at his hungry and freezing people. He knew that the end had come. Sorrowfully,

he led them back on the last long march to the Red
Cloud Reservation.

But the Indian Affairs people in Washington were
still afraid of Crazy Horse. Orders went out to the
reservation that he was to be arrested on arrival. He
would not have a trial, and was to be imprisoned for
life in the Dry Tortugas, a small island chain off the
coast of Florida which was a federal prison camp.

None of the soldiers had the courage to tell Crazy
Horse that he had already been sentenced. He was

and all the rights and privileges in Nebraska, and on the Republican Fork, of the Smoky Hill River, secured to us by said treaty.

    Provided – That we do not surrender any right of occupation of the country situated in Nebraska, North, of the Divide, which is south of, and near to the Niobrara River, and West of the 100th Meridian; but desire to retain that country for future occupation and use.

Little his x mark Wound,	Taopi Chikila	Chief
Pawnee his x mark Killer	Stili kta	Sub-Chief
Black his x mark Bear	Mato Sape	Sub-Chief
Iron his x mark Horse	Ta dunkamaza	Soldier
Quick his x mark Bear	Mato luza	Sub-Chief
Red his x mark Dog	Xunkaluta	Chief
High his x mark Wolf	Xunka manito wakanto	Chief
Conquering his x mark Bear	Mato yui	Head Soldier
White Crane his x mark Walking	Pahasa mani	Head Soldier
Tail his x mark Lance	Wahukeza Wakatia	Soldier
Bear's his x mark Robe	Mato ha xina	Soldier
Red his x mark Leaf	Warpexa	Chief
Day his mark	Ampaha	Chief
Yellow his x mark Hair	Pehizizi	Head Soldier
White his x mark Tail	Sin teska	Sub-Chief

simply asked to call on the reservation's commanding officer.

Not until Crazy Horse was inside the Army barracks did he see the barred windows and realize that he was in jail. With a war yell, he broke away from the soldiers who were escorting him and made a dash for the door.

The officer of the guard shouted: "Stab him! Kill him!"

A soldier lunged forward with his bayonet and sank it hilt-deep between Crazy Horse's ribs. Slowly he collapsed to the wooden floor. The great fighting chief of the Oglala Sioux was dead. The next morning he was to be buried in the reservation graveyard.

But late that night, some of his Oglala people threw his body over the back of a horse, slipped past the military guard, and headed toward the Black Hills.

No one knows the location of Crazy Horse's grave. But somewhere his body is resting beneath the soil of the sacred hunting grounds of the Sioux that he had fought so long and so hard to save.

"SIGN OR STARVE!"

On the facing page is a copy of the final treaty by which the Sioux ceded the Black Hills to the United States. The Indians had no choice in the matter. The commissioners gave them an ultimatum: "Sign or starve!" In the left-hand column are the Indians' English names. The middle is the phonetic spelling of their names in the Sioux tongue. The column on the right indicates their tribal rank.

°☉°

CHAPTER THREE

~~~~~~~~~~~~~~~~~~~~~~~~~~~

CHIEF JOSEPH

◆

MAN OF PEACE—AND WAR

CHIEF JOSEPH HAS BEEN CALLED THE "MOST BRILLIANT of all Western Indian chiefs." He was a member of the Nez Percé, an advanced and unusual Indian tribe that lived in the lovely Wallowa Valley—the Valley of the Winding Waters—which lies between the Blue and the Bitter Root Mountains on the borders of what are now Oregon, Washington, and Idaho.

The Nez Percé were a friendly and peace-loving peo-ple. They welcomed the first white settlers and mis-

CHIEF JOSEPH

sionaries who came West, and were eager to learn the white man's ways. Most of them, including young Joseph, became Christians, and many gave up their Indian names and adopted Christian ones.

Joseph's original name was Hin-mah-too-yah-laht-ket, meaning Thunder Rolling in the Mountains. He renamed himself Joseph when he entered a Christian mission school as a small boy.

In 1855, Joseph's father, old Tu-eka-kas, had been one of the chiefs who signed a treaty with the government in Washington which gave away most of the land between the Blues and the Bitter Roots to white settlement. But he had refused to leave the Wallowa and move his people to a reservation. The Agency for Indian Affairs felt that it had made a good enough bargain and accepted Tu-eka-kas's terms.

However, eight years later, the Agency called another meeting with the Nez Percé. More immigrants had been coming to the Northwest, and once again the tribe was ordered to move out of their beloved Valley of the Winding Waters and go to the reservation at Lapwai.

Young Joseph, who attended the council in place of his ailing father, refused to sign. Some of the other Nez Percé chiefs gave in. But Joseph went back to his

own band and warned the white settlers to stay away. The government still did not want to stir up too much trouble with these Indians who, up to now, had been so friendly and unwarlike. They took no action against Joseph. But ranchers began moving into the blossoming grasslands of the Wallowa, and there were a few fights.

Upon the death of his father, in 1871, young Joseph officially became Chief Joseph. As chief, he held firmly to his policy of nonviolent resistance to Washington's orders. On one occasion, a Nez Percé tribesman was killed by a white settler who was later hunted down and captured by an Indian scouting party. The man was brought before Joseph for sentencing.

"I will not kill," Joseph declared firmly. "My sentence is that this man shall go free."

At last, in 1873, President Ulysses S. Grant issued an order that the Valley of the Winding Waters rightfully and for all time belonged to the Nez Percé, and that it would not be used for white settlement.

Joseph and his people were happy and content. They thought that their troubles were at last over. But their troubles were only beginning. The white farmers and ranchers refused to move out of the Wallowa and even more came pouring in. There were clashes between Nez Percé warriors and white settlers, which resulted in a few killings on both sides. But through it all, Joseph stood steadfast, doing everything in his power to keep a truce.

Meanwhile, President Grant's decision that Wallowa belonged exclusively to the Nez Percé had been meeting with protests from Congress, from the Indian Agency, and from the great numbers of settlers who wanted to take over the fertile Valley of the Winding

Waters. Two years after he had issued the order, Grant bowed to the tremendous pressure and canceled it.

General Oliver O. Howard, commander of the U.S. Army in the Northwest, asked Joseph for a pow-wow at Lapwai. He explained the government's position, but Joseph once again refused to move his tribe to the reservation.

"We lived in peace until the white man came," he said. "We have never made war against the white man. We love this land. It is our home. We will never give it up."

In his report of the meeting, General Howard wrote to the President: "I believe it is a grave mistake to take the Wallowa Valley from Chief Joseph and his peaceful Nez Percé." But this advice was ignored. Howard was ordered to go back and tell Joseph that if he did not bring his people to the reservation, the Army would take them in by force.

Joseph knew that the United States Army outnumbered his own braves by ten or twenty to one. He also knew that the Blue Coats were armed with new repeating rifles, while his warriors had only bows and arrows and a few old-fashioned muskets. Sadly he agreed to Howard's demand.

"Rather than go to war," he said, "I would give

59

up my country. I would give up everything."

He was allowed just one month to move all his people to the Lapwai Reservation. This was in April of 1877.

When the white ranchers learned that Joseph and his tribe were finally leaving the Valley of the Winding Waters, a few hotheads organized a raid on the Nez Percé horse herds and made off with several hundred prize stallions and mares. Some of Joseph's young braves, burning to fight back, put on their war paint without Joseph's knowledge and attacked two ranches. They killed half a dozen cowhands and came riding back into camp whooping and waving the scalps of the dead palefaces over their heads.

This, Joseph realized, meant that all of his hopes and attempts to keep the peace had come to an end. As chief, he would be blamed for the killings. And he was certain that Howard's army would be coming after him. Now there was no choice except war.

When the man of peace was forced to turn into a man of war, he displayed a natural talent for miltary matters that historians have compared with that of the world's greatest generals.

Joseph knew that he had no chance of defeating General Howard's army in open battle. Therefore he decided to take his tribe—which numbered about 500

women and children, and some 300 warriors—to join
Sitting Bull in Canada. The Sioux chief had gone there
with his Hunkpapa after the Custer battle. Joseph got
as far as White Bird Canyon in Idaho, where the White
Bird Creek flows into the Salmon River, when his
scouts informed him that the Blue Coats were coming.

Moving the women and children safely out of the
way, Joseph lined up his fighters behind the rocks and
outcroppings of the canyon walls.

"Take no scalps," he ordered. "Only weapons and
ammunition."

In all the battles and skirmishes that he fought, Joseph gave strict orders that there should be no scalping. And there was none.

When Colonel David Perry and his troopers of the First Cavalry rode into the canyon at early dawn of June 17, Joseph's braves swarmed in on them. A third of the soldiers were killed by Nez Percé arrows almost before they knew what hit them. The rest scattered and tried to reform, but Joseph kept up his attack and they retreated back to their fort at Mount Idaho.

A few days later, scouts brought word that General Howard was coming with a force of Horse Soldiers twice the size of Perry's. Joseph crossed the low foothills of the Bitter Roots to the Clearwater River. There he outflanked the American cavalry and forced Howard to divide his forces. The Army's lines of communication and supplies were cut off. Once again, the Americans retreated.

During the next four months, Joseph fought back and forth across more than 2,000 miles of rugged, mountainous country. In a dozen or more engagements with five different Army columns, he outgeneraled General Howard. He made secret night raids—a new tactic, since Indians had never fought at night and the Army felt secure after the sun had gone down. He ran off or stole whole herds of Army horses and mules, leaving the cavalry without any means of transportation. He hit Army patrols when they thought he was hundreds of miles away. All the time, he was slowly heading toward the safety of Canada.

At Big Hole, in the heart of the Bitter Roots, Joseph met defeat for the first time. An Army regiment, coming west from Montana, caught the Nez Percé sleeping wearily in their teepee camp and managed to kill about half of them, mostly women and children, before Joseph's braves could rally and drive them back.

Still, Chief Joseph kept heading north—up the Bitter Roots, over the Lolo Pass, across the Rockies, through the Yellowstone and into the Bear Paw Mountains. But when every battle was over, there were fewer and fewer warriors left to fight.

The final clash came only about thirty miles from the safety of the Canadian border. General Nelson Miles, with a large force of cavalry, succeeded in cutting Joseph off at Eagle Creek, in Montana. Miles sent a scout under a white flag into the Nez Percé camp to demand an immediate surrender.

It was now October. The season of snows and blizzards had begun. It was bitterly cold, and Joseph had no wood for fires, nor any blankets or food for his people. Only eighty-seven of his warriors were left alive, and of these more than half were wounded so badly that they could not bend a bow or fire a rifle. Most of the women and children were so ill that they could hardly be moved. It was the bitter end of the trail.

Joseph rode out of his camp to meet General Miles. His head was bowed, and his shoulders were covered with a shabby blanket. He handed his rifle to the general.

"My people are starving," he said to Miles. "I have no food to give them. They are freezing and we have few blankets. I have fought, but I am tired of fighting. From where the sun now stands, Joseph will fight no more, forever."

Chapter Three: *CHIEF JOSEPH*

General Miles promised that what was left of the Nez Percé would be returned to the reservation at Lapwai.

But this was not to be, even though the general protested to Washington. Joseph and his remaining Nez Percé were taken to the bottomlands of Kansas. Unaccustomed to the low country, many of them died. Later they were transferred to the even worse wastelands of Oklahoma. There the bone-dry climate all but wiped out what was left of the once-proud Nez Percé.

In 1897, Chief Joseph traveled to Washington to plead the case of his people with President Rutherford B. Hayes. He was the houseguest of General Miles, who was then commander-in-chief of the Army. The general was still trying to make good his pledge that the Nez Percé would be allowed to live in their old home in the Valley of the Winding Waters.

Miles wrote to Indian Agency officials: "These people have been loyal to the government and friends of the white race from the time their country was first explored. Chief Joseph, in his skillful campaigns, has spared hundreds of lives and thousands of dollars' worth of property that he might have destroyed. The Nez Percé have been badly wronged."

From Washington, Joseph went to New York. Everywhere he appeared he was received with honors. Buffalo Bill Cody's Wild West Show was then playing in New York's Madison Square Garden. When the old chief rode around the ring in a carriage with Colonel Cody, he received a standing ovation.

As a result of this trip to the East, most of the surviving Nez Percé were returned to the Valley of the Winding Waters. But Joseph himself, for some reason that no one knows, was never allowed to go back. Instead, he was sent to the Colville Reservation in the state of Washington.

There he settled down to becoming an old man, uninterested in what went on in the outside world. And there, on the evening of September 21, 1904, as he sat near his campfire, his broken heart stopped beating. He fell forward, lifeless, toward the embers of the dying fire.

A newspaper reporter named Charles Erskine Wood, who had been present when the chief surrendered to General Miles, wrote the final word about Joseph and the Nez Percé

"I think that in his long career, Chief Joseph of the Nez Percé could not accuse the government of the United States of one single act of justice."

CHAPTER FOUR

SITTING BULL

CHIEF AND MEDICINE MAN

AS IS THE CASE WITH MOST EARLY INDIAN CHIEFS, NOT
very much is known about the childhood and the youth-
ful years of Sitting Bull. A Hunkpapa Sioux, he was
born about 1830 somewhere on the great Plains of what
are now Wyoming and the Dakotas.

Sitting Bull's original name was Hunkeshnee, meaning "slow," because even as a youngster he was slower
than most Indians in both his speech and his actions.
But according to a story that he later told, when he was

SITTING BULL

about twelve he and some other boys of his own age tagged along after a buffalo-hunting party. When the hunt was finished, and the Hunkpapa had killed all the buffalo they needed, the boys amused themselves by chasing a group of buffalo calves that had been separated from the main herd. Acting suddenly, he leaped up on the back of the biggest buffalo calf and hauled back on its ears until he forced it to sit down on its haunches. From then on he was called Sitting Bull.

Like all Indian boys, Sitting Bull was trained to be a warrior. But in later years, when the Plains Wars were in their fiercest stages, it was as a medicine man and inspirational leader that he earned the fame that has put his name into the history books.

Because he had shown outstanding qualities of leadership as a young man, he was chosen chief of the Hunkpapa Sioux while only in his twenties. In the long struggle with the army that followed the breaking of the Powder River treaty, it was Sitting Bull who was the master planner while Crazy Horse was the fighting war chief.

In the beginning, when the first wave of white immigrants began streaming over the Oregon Trail, Sitting Bull tried to keep the peace by avoiding them. He pulled his people back into the Black Hills and the Powder

River Country. The Washington government had guaranteed this land to them, and the buffalo hunting was good there.

"This land is big," Sitting Bull said to the Hunkpapa. "There is room for all."

During the few years of peace that followed while the Powder River treaty was in effect, Sitting Bull began an unusual project. He started writing his autobiography. He did this, not with symbols such as Sequoyah had invented, but in a series of colored drawings, each drawing showing a high point in his life. He drew them in the pages of a book which he had bought from a passing trader. (This rare book, which was stolen by an American soldier during Sitting Bull's imprisonment and rediscovered long afterward quite by accident, is now a priceless historical relic.)

But the peaceful times in the Powder River Country were not to last for long. Homesteaders streamed into the Plains. The railroads stretched out their lines of steel across the Indians' land. Gold seekers flocked into the Black Hills. Indians, everywhere, were ordered to reservations. Now Sitting Bull felt that peace with the white men was no longer possible.

Bull—as he was usually referred to by American soldiers—called for a council of war. Leaders of the Cheyenne and Arapaho, as well as the Sioux, came to listen to his advice.

"The whites want war," he told the assembled chiefs. "I will seek a vision to see whether or not we should give it to them."

To make "big medicine," Bull ordered that one hundred cuts be made in his arms and shoulders. Then he sat facing the sun until he fainted from loss of blood. When he finally revived, he proclaimed that the gods had shown him a dream. In it, he saw thousands of Blue Coats coming into the Sioux camp upside down. This meant, he said, that an Indian victory was certain. He and Crazy Horse, along with the other chiefs, decided to fight.

But the sad fact is that they succeeded too well. With the defeat of Custer at the Little Big Horn—in the very month that Americans were celebrating their first hundred years of independence—the Indians actually lost their war by winning the battle.

The huge American Army began hunting them down without mercy. It was then that Bull gave up what he knew at last to be a hopeless cause and led his tribe to the safety of Canada.

Life in Canada was peaceful, but it was hard. The Red Coats (as the Sioux called the Canadian Mounties) promised to give them a home as long as they did not make trouble by raiding white ranchers and stealing horses. But there were no buffalo north of the border. Sitting Bull had to send hunting parties back into the northern United States to look for the few remaining buffalo so that they would have meat for food and hides for trading. There they ran into patrols of American cavalry and had to fight their way back.

It was not long before Bull and his half-starved tribe

became too much of a headache for Canadian officials. They urged him to take his people back to a reservation in the States. After all, they argued, he was the last holdout among the Plains tribes. Crazy Horse and Chief Joseph had given up. The day of the free Indian, they told him, was finished. The old chief soon realized that it would not be long before the Canadians would force him to go whether he wanted to or not.

Finally, in July of 1881, he took his tribe back across the border and surrendered.

He had been told that if he gave himself up peacefully he would be fully pardoned, and given a piece of land on the Standing Rock Reservation in Dakota. Instead, he was immediately arrested as the killer of Colonel Cody and sent to prison at Fort Randall. There the Army officers, who respected Sitting Bull for his military leadership, treated him well. After two years, he was allowed to rejoin his people at Standing Rock. Although the Indian Agency did not recognize him as a chief, the Hunkpapa continued to look upon him as their leader and adviser. He tried to lead them wisely and well.

For one season he traveled through the East with Buffalo Bill's Wild West Show, where he was the star attraction. He learned to scribble his name in English,

and made a good deal of money by selling his autograph to the curious Easterners. But he gave all the money to his tribe. When the show closed at the end of the summer, Buffalo Bill took him to Washington to meet the President before his return to Standing Rock.

But Sitting Bull was not content to be a reservation Indian. Although he was now getting old, his thoughts were always back on the open Plains, as the Plains had been in his youth. He did not like the reservation food, which was tasteless compared with rich buffalo meat. He did not like being cooped up, unable to roam over the country whenever he wished. But most of all he did not like to see the young people of his tribe brought up in the white man's ways.

Then a strange thing happened that put new heart into the Western Indians locked up in their reservations. A Paiute medicine man named Wovoka claimed to have had a vision. In it, he said, he had been transported to heaven, where the Great Spirit told him that the power of the white men would soon be destroyed, that the Indians would return to their old life, and that the buffalo would again be as thick on the Plains as stars in the Milky Way. But for all this to come about, the Indians must follow a new religion that expressed itself in the Ghost Dance. The holy symbol of the Ghost Dance was the Ghost Shirt. When a warrior was wearing this shirt, Wovoka said, bullets from the white man's guns could not harm them.

The Ghost Dance swept through the Great Plains like a prairie fire. Young braves began jumping the reservations, and the Army became alarmed.

Sitting Bull had no faith in this new religion. But the Army and the officials of the Indian Agency still remembered him as the chief who had planned the massacre of Custer and his men. They believed that Bull was one of the Ghost Dance leaders. They ordered his arrest.

On the night of December 15, 1890, a squad of reservation police went to his cabin to arrest him. Sitting Bull tried to explain that he did not believe in the new religion and had taken no part in it. While he was attempting to argue with the police, one of them suddenly pulled out his pistol and pumped several shots into Sitting Bull's body, killing him instantly.

One last note—

Two weeks later, the Ghost Dance religion came to a quick and sad end at Wounded Knee Creek in the Dakota Badlands. Here a cavalry unit had rounded up a large number of Indians who had fled the reservations. A few of the warriors, certain that their Ghost Shirts would protect them from harm, opened fire on the soldiers. The cavalry replied with bursts from their repeating rifles and the newly invented Hotchkiss machine gun. When it was all over, more than two hundred Indians lay dead in front of their teepees.

This was the final resistance of the Plains Indians to their white conquerors. From then on there was only one road open to them—the white man's road.

Stephen Vincent Benét, the famous American poet, sang the death song of the Plains Indians when he ended a poem with this line:

Bury my heart at Wounded Knee.

GERONIMO

LAST OF THE FIGHTING APACHE

WHENEVER PARATROOPERS OF THE UNITED STATES Army Airborne Command jump into battle, each man, as he steps out the open door of the airplane, yells at the top of his voice: *"Geronimo! Geronimo!"*

This was the war cry of the Apache, the most feared Indians in the history of the Southwest. And Geronimo, the last of their fighting "war chiefs," was the most fearsome fighter of them all.

When Geronimo was born in the bleak desert country of Arizona, in 1829, his mother named him Gokliya, which meant "He-Who-Yawns." But like most Indians, he later took another name. It was Mexican soldiers who renamed him Geronimo.

The Arizona of that day was a dry wasteland of deserts, canyons, and rocky hills. Water was scarce, and there were few flowing streams. Here and there lay scattered valleys of lush meadows and woods that were full of buffalo, elk, deer, wild turkey, and other game. But these were few and far between. Yet the Apache managed to live well by sending regular hunting parties into these valleys from their desert homes.

The first white men that the Apache ever saw were the Spanish soldiers of Don Francisco Vásquez de Coronado who, in 1540, set out from Mexico City in search of the fabled "Seven cities of gold." The Conquistadores had heard legends that these cities, which were supposed to lie somewhere to the north, were so rich that people used gold to make their everyday tools, and that precious gem stones were as easy to find as pebbles. Of course, no such golden cities existed. But Coronado believed that the Indians were keeping the location of these cities a secret. To get the secret out of them, his men captured hundreds of Apaches and other Southwest Indians, and tortured and killed them.

GERONIMO

Chapter Five: GERONIMO

The senseless cruelty of these early Spaniards caused the Apache to develop a bitter hatred of all white men, a hatred that lasted for three and a half centuries.

At the time of Geronimo's birth, Arizona was a part of Mexico. Mexican miners dug for copper in the desert. Mexican settlers moved in to hunt for game in the forests and set up cattle ranches in the grassy valleys. The Apache, having always been a warlike tribe, fought back to protect their homeland. They raided mining camps and ranches, ambushed supply trains, and killed every Mexican they captured. The Mexican soldiers were no match for the fighting Apache.

In 1848, after the United States had won the Mexican War, the government in Washington claimed all the Southwest as American territory. A flood of white immigrants rushed in. Some were on their way to the gold fields of California. But hundreds stayed in the Apache's country and took over the old Mexican ranches and mines. The Apache fought the White Eyes, as they called the Americans, just as they had the Mexicans.

By this time Geronimo had become a young subchief. He was reckless and without fear. The older chiefs appointed him the fighting commander of all the Apache warrior-braves.

The American victory in the Mexican War gave Geronimo and his warriors one big benefit. Up until then, the Apache had raided from Arizona and New Mexico to the Sierra Madre Mountains in Old Mexico. Now a new international boundary between the two countries had been surveyed. Geronimo soon discovered that if he and his braves staged a raid on the United States' side of the line, they had only to slip across the border and the Blue Coats would not be allowed to follow.

American troops came storming into Apache country to stand guard over the new settlers. It did not take long for Geronimo to learn how to outwit and outfight the Horse Soldiers.

After the American occupation of the Southwest, the Apache had little trouble with the Mexicans south of the new border. When the Apache had a good hunting season, they made peaceful trading trips to Mexican towns.

On one such occasion, the entire Apache-Bedonko band, of which Geronimo was a member, made a trek into Mexico. The men who had furs and skins to trade rode into town. The rest of the band camped outside in the desert.

Unknown to the Apache, the government of Mexico had offered a bounty for every Apache scalp. It would pay one hundred dollars for the scalp of every Apache brave; fifty dollars for a woman's scalp; and twenty-five dollars for that of a child.

While Geronimo and his men were inside the town making their trades, a group of Mexican soldiers slipped out to the Indian encampment. There they killed and scalped everyone. Among the dead was Geronimo's young wife.

Late that evening when the braves returned to the camp, they were stunned by the horrible sight that greeted them. Geronimo and the other young men screamed for immediate vengeance. But old Mangas Coloradas, the senior chief, counseled patience.

"We will go home," he said, "and get the help of the Mescalero and the Chiricahua." These were other Apache bands. "Then we will return in force and destroy this town. We will take fifty lives for every one we have lost."

When all the Apache had gathered, Mangas and Cochise, who was chief of the Chiricahua, appointed Geronimo to lead the attackers. Returning to Mexico, the warriors hid themselves in a gully outside the town. Using an old Indian trick, Geronimo sent out a dozen braves to show themselves and make the Mexican soldiers show their positions. When the Mexicans took the bait, the Apache swarmed out from their hiding places and pounced on them. Recognizing the Indian leader, the Mexicans ran for their lives, shouting: *"Geronimo! Geronimo!"* The Apache took up the cry, *"Geronimo! Geronimo!"* as they rode after the fleeing soldiers. They killed every one, and burned the town.

From that time on, *"Geronimo! Geronimo!"* was the Apache battle cry.

By 1861, several thousand immigrants had moved into Arizona and New Mexico. But with the opening shots of the Civil War, the Army regiments left the frontier forts to fight the Confederates. The settlers had to take care of themselves. The Apache burned the empty forts. They raided and looted the scattered ranches, homesteads, and small towns. The frightened settlers left their homes and scurried to the safety of Tucson, the only big fortress-town in the territory.

For the next four years, the Apache lived in their old ways, alone and unbothered in their native homeland. But after the Civil War, the United States Army returned. The soldiers had orders to capture all Apache women and children, but to shoot any Apache male, old or young, on sight. The Army's rule was: "The only good Apache is a dead Apache. Let's make 'em all good!"

The Apache raids resumed, although with more care. But Mangas Coloradas, the aging chief, figured that there were too many soldiers fighting his people. Without consulting any of his fellow chiefs, he went alone into an Army encampment to try to arrange a truce. He was shot and killed, "while trying to escape" according to the official report.

Geronimo, who succeeded Mangas as chief, left his

old home in the desert and joined Cochise in his stronghold in the Chiricahua Mountains. As revenge for the murder of Mangas, black smoke from dozens of burning ranch houses darkened the yellow Arizona sky. But more and more soldiers poured into the Southwest. At last Cochise, who was growing old and tired of fighting, agreed to a peace parley.

If the Apache would stop their raiding, he was told, they could keep their old lands as a reservation. Cochise signed the treaty, but Geronimo angrily turned his back on the council fire and walked away. Followed by a hundred or so braves, and as many women, he vanished into the hills.

For a time, the "tamed" Apache were treated well and fairly. Many of the former warriors joined up with the Army as scouts. But, as was the case with the Sioux and the Nez Percé, the growing number of white immigrants began to put pressure on Congress, the Agency for Indian Affairs, and President Grant to allow them to settle on Apache land. Once again, the President bowed to their demands. All the Apache were ordered to the San Carlos Reservation, in the most barren corner of the Arizona desert.

On the march to San Carlos, a great many of the braves lost hope and slipped away to join Geronimo.

His force grew to about three hundred warriors. With them, he began to raid on both sides of the border—killing, looting, and capturing all the guns and ammunition he could lay his hands on. But an Army force, more than ten times the size of his, was always on his trail.

Geronimo led the cavalry a merry chase. He raided in Arizona, then hopped across the line where the American Army could not follow. A few days later, he would stage a raid on a Mexican border town, and quickly escape to the United States. After a few months of this confusion, Mexico and the United States joined

in what was called a "hot trail treaty." This allowed American troops to cross over into Mexican territory any time they were after Geronimo.

By the spring of 1883, this cat-and-mouse game was wearing the Apache down. Geronimo now had only fifty-two braves left. Half of them were wounded and unable to fight. He also had two hundred and seventy-three women and children. The band was much too difficult to organize for such hop-and-skip antics. Geronimo sent a runner to the reservation to make a deal and gave himself up and took his people to San Carlos. There he was given the best farm on the reservation. The entire Army sighed with relief. At last the Apache wars were over. From now on Geronimo and his warriors "would be raising corn instead of scalps."

Some of the Apache grew to like the easy life on the reservation. But Geronimo grew restless again. Almost two years after he had surrendered, he gathered together a small group of warriors, stole Army horses and supplies, and skipped the reservation. He led his small army back to the Sierra Madres, where he had stored guns and ammunition. Then he began his raids all over again.

Now headlines in newspapers all over the country screamed for his capture: GERONIMO ON THE WARPATH

Chapter Five: GERONIMO

AGAIN! Who was this fabulous fighting Indian, they demanded, who could defy the might of the entire United States Army?

General Nelson A. Miles, commander of the Army of the Southwest, organized a chase. He had 5,000 soldiers and 500 friendly Indian scouts. But Geronimo refused to let up. He raided ranches, ran off horses and cattle, and cut the Army's telegraph wires. No rancher felt safe. There was no way of telling where he might hit next.

Finally, by July of 1866, he had only 18 able-bodied men against 5,000 soldiers. He arranged a surrender. This time for good.

Geronimo and all the other Apache at San Carlos were sent to a reservation in the south of Florida. In the hot, humid air of the subtropics, his people died like flies. At last, the tribe was shipped back to the Fort Sill Reservation in Oklahoma. There Geronimo settled down on a small farm to live out the rest of his life.

But in spite of the fact that he and his warriors had burned and looted hundreds of ranches and towns, and killed scores of people, Geronimo became a legendary hero. He was a much-sought-after attraction at circuses and world fairs. He sold pictures of himself, and

made enough money to buy a big automobile which he proudly learned to drive. Oftentimes, he wore a tailcoat and a high silk hat.

Then came the crowning honor of his life, just four years before his death at the age of eighty.

When Theodore Roosevelt was reelected President of the United States in 1904, he invited Geronimo to come to Washington as his guest for the inaugural celebration. In his youth, Roosevelt had been a Western rancher and Indian fighter.

As the inaugural procession made its way down Pennsylvania Avenue from the Capitol to the White House, thousands of cheering people lined the streets. Hundreds of flags flew. Companies of soldiers marched along as honor guards. Roosevelt stood up in his carriage, flashed his famous big-toothed grin, and waved to the crowd.

Then, behind the Presidential carriage, rode the old Apache chief. He sat ramrod-straight on a paint pony that danced and pranced over the pavement. He wore a buckskin jacket, fringed pants, and an eagle feather in his headband. His face was streaked with war paint.

And as he passed, the people on the sidewalks paid him a last triumphant tribute. With one great voice they began to shout the old Apache war cry:

"Geronimo! Geronimo!"

INDEX